Elementare Bauformen

Elemental Building Forms

Baumeisterforum

Werner Blaser

Elementare Bauformen

Quellen moderner Architektur

Werner Blaser

Elemental Building Forms

Sources of Modern Architecture

Beton-Verlag

720
B64e

CIP-Kurztitelaufnahme der Deutschen Bibliothek

Blaser, Werner:
Elementare Bauformen: Quellen moderner Architektur =
Elemental building forms / Werner Blaser. –
Düsseldorf: Beton-Verlag, 1982.
  (Baumeisterforum; 2)
   ISBN 3-7640-0166-6
NE: GT

© by Beton-Verlag GmbH, Düsseldorf, 1982
Satz: tgr gmbh, Remscheid
Druck und Verarbeitung: Boss-Druck, Kleve
Reproduktionen: K. Urlichs, Düsseldorf

English version: D. O. Stephenson

Vorwort

Foreword

Um alle Mißverständnisse und fehlbasierende Diskussionen von vornherein auszuschließen, sei vermerkt, daß diese Arbeit eine subjektive Darstellung ist. Es geht im Prinzip darum, in Wort und vor allem im Bild für die gerade heute so notwendig gewordene Besinnung auf das Wesen der Architektur, auf ihren Wert und ihren Sinn für ein menschliches Leben einen Beitrag zu leisten. Nicht nur das Resultat, sondern mehr noch die Überzeugungskraft und Folgerichtigkeit der Ideen beinhaltet diese Arbeit an erster Stelle und fördert so das Verständnis, was Architektur ist und was sie uns auch heute zu sagen hat.

Wiederum besorgte Walter Grunder, Photograph, sämtliche Vergrößerungen, ausgehend von meinem 6 × 6 Negativmaterial.

Ganz besonders danke ich Martin Erny, der bei meinen Arbeiten und Projekten wesentlich mitbeteiligt war. Den Kollegen Helmut Jahn, Florian Vischer und Georges Weber, Friedrich Kurrent und Johannes Spalt, sowie Livio Vacchini danke ich für Planunterlagen. Sämtliche Zeichnungen wurden aus den in der Bibliographie angegebenen Büchern entnommen.

Die beiden Titelbilder zeigen Bauen mit Gestalt; der volkstümlichen, elementaren Architektur im Val Verzasca (Tessin) steht Frank Lloyd Wrights Bauwerk gegenüber.

In order to rule out from the outset all misconceptions and discussions based on false premises it should be emphasized that this work represents a subjective account. It is concerned in principle with marshalling arguments in both words and pictures for an appraisal, so urgently necessary in these days, of the nature of architecture, and of its value and purpose in human life. This aspect must be seen quite separately from whatever modest instructive value the pictures may have with which the work is documented. In certain examples there are links with more than one theme. The book is more than just the sum total of the results of the survey; it is concerned rather to present persuasively and with logical consistency ideas on what architecture really is and what message it holds for us today.

Once again Walter Grunder, photographer, saw to all the enlargements made from 6 x 6 negatives.

I am indebted to my colleagues Helmut Jahn, Florian Vischer and Georges Weber, Friedrich Kurrent and Johannes Spalt, and Livio Vacchini for plans. I am particularly grateful to Martin Erny, who was closely associated with my works and projects. All the drawings were taken from the books given in the Bibliography.

The two photographs on the jacket show buildings informed with a sense of design: the simple vernacular architecture in the Val Verzasca (Ticino) is paralleled by Frank Lloyd Wright's building.

Basel, im August 1982   Werner Blaser

Inhalt

Contents

Einführung	8

I.
Alt und neu im Dialog — 9

1. Anpassung an Vorhandenes	10
Alte Universität am Rheinsprung Basel	10
Zentralsparkasse Florisdorf in Wien	12
Anbauprojekt Haus Steiner in Küsnacht	14
2. Vom Raum zur Raumdurchdringung	16
Piazza Grande in Locarno	16
Minnesota Capitol Complex − Projekt	18
Neugestaltung Barfüsserplatz in Basel	20
3. Addierte Elemente der Baugestalt	22
Fabrikgebäude in Bern	22
St. Antoniuskirche in Basel	24
Casa Nascosta in Ascona	26

II.
Bewährte Elemente der Architektur — 29

1. Elementare Architektur	30
Le Village des Bories in Gordes	31
Bauformen auf Irland und den Aran-Inseln	44
Walser-Häuser aus Alagna Valsesia	56
2. Tradierte Architektur	68
Blockbauten aus der Region Maramures	69
Mediterrane Architektur auf Stromboli	82
Bauernhäuser im Burgenland	94
3. Expressive Architektur	106
Piemontesischer Barock von Bernardo A. Vittone	107
Klassizistische Architektur in Naantali	120
Dachformen von Frank Lloyd Wright	132
Schrifttum	142
Nachweis der Zeichnungen	142
Index	143
Karte von Europa	144

Prefatory note	8

I.
Old and new in dialogue — 9

1. Adaptation to the existing	10
Old university on the Rheinsprung, Basle	10
Florisdorf Savings Bank, Vienna	12
Addition to the Steiner house at Küsnacht	14
2. From space to spatial interpenetration	16
Piazza Grande at Locarno	16
Minnesota Capitol Complex − Project	18
Redesign of the Barfüsserplatz in Basle	20
3. Added elements of architectural design	22
Factory building in Berne	22
Church of St. Antonius in Basle	24
Casa Nascosta at Ascona	26

II.
Proven elements of architecture — 29

1. Indigenous architecture	30
Le village des Bories at Gordes	31
Building forms in Ireland and on the Aran Isles	44
Walser houses from Alagna Valsesia	56
2. Vernacular architecture	68
Log constructions from the region of Maramureş	69
Mediterranean architecture on Stromboli	82
Farmhouses in Burgenland	94
3. Expressive architecture	106
Piedmontese Baroque of Bernardo A. Vittone	107
Neo-classical architecture at Naantali	120
Roof designs by Frank Lloyd Wright	132
Bibliography	142
Sources of drawings	142
Index	143
Map of Europe	144

Einführung

Prefatory note

Dieses Buch befaßt sich mit elementaren Hausformen, gezeigt an historischen Beispielen von Barock bis Klassizismus und an Werken des zwanzigsten Jahrhunderts. Die ausgewählten Beispiele zeigen den Dialog zwischen Vergangenheit und Gegenwart. Es geht dabei nicht um nostalgische Neuigkeiten oder fremdländische Kuriosa, sondern um die erneuerte Begegnung mit Werken von gestern, die auch heute noch Gültigkeit haben und bei denen die Verkörperung von Ordnung und Schönheit in Konstruktion und Material am klarsten durchgeführt wurde. Bewährte Elemente der Architektur vermögen gerade unserer Modernität einen starken Akzent zu geben.

Im Vorspann wird die Problemstellung „alt und neu im Dialog" umrissen: ein Aufbruch zu neuen Idealen aus der Sichtbarmachung von alten Normen und Werten, die auch für unser Schaffen gültig sind. Gezeigt werden Werke, die aus diesem Dialog heraus entstanden sind und die eine Verschmelzung von alter Bausubstanz und neuer Aufgabe herbeigeführt haben.

Der Hauptteil zeigt Beispiele alter Architekturelemente in zahlreichen Bildern. Die drei Kapitel widmen sich jeweils einem Thema: In der elementar-atavistischen Architektur finden wir das Ursprüngliche, aber auch Anregungen für Gestaltideen unter der Berücksichtigung von Grundsatzfragen, wie etwas gemacht wird und von welcher Bedeutung etwas für uns sein kann. Die tradiert-volkstümliche Architektur ist der Bereich des Vertrauten, wobei Tradition und Fortschritt einander keineswegs ausschließen. Bei der expressiv-plastischen Architektur im dritten Abschnitt wird die ausdrucksbetonte Gestalt sichtbar, als eine vom Architekten zusätzlich eingebrachte Qualität. Daraus können sich Möglichkeiten für neue spontane Tendenzen ergeben.

Gesehenes, Gedachtes, Geplantes, Gemachtes bestimmen das Nachdenken eines Architekten über Architektur. Es soll zum Ausdruck kommen, wie ein Architekt Bauten anschaut, sie auf eigenen Fotos festhält und in ihnen Prinzipien und Gesetze erkennt. Es sollen Gestaltungsprozesse dargestellt und somit die architektonische Gestalt aufgewertet werden.

This book deals with elemental forms of houses and shows historical examples from Baroque to Classicism, and buildings from the twentieth century. All these examples have been chosen because they represent a dialogue between the past and the present. We are not concerned with nostalgic novelties or with exotic curiosities but rather with renewing acquaintance with works of yesterday which are still valid for us today and in which order and beauty have been embodied in construction and material with exemplary clarity. Such elements of architecture as these are precisely what should feature prominently in our "modernity".

In the introduction we shall consider the problem presented by "old and new in dialogue": Standards and values, when their principles are compared and contrasted, furnish us with a new ideal to guide us in our work.

The main section is divided into three chapters, each with three basic themes, and takes the form of a systematic analysis of constructional principles. In the most unsophisticated form of building bound to indigenous customs and materials we find what is original and basic but at the same time we meet with suggestions of how design problems can be tackled, bearing in mind the fundamentals of architecture, and see how something is done and what significance it has for us. With vernacular architecture we enter the sphere of the familiar where tradition and progress are by no means mutually exclusive. In the expressive "sculptured" building, design as a medium of expression comes into prominence and figures as an additional quality conferred by the architect. This again is full of potentialities for new and spontaneous trends.

What has been seen, thought, planned and fashioned shapes the meditations of an architect on architecture. The aim is to show how an architect looks at buildings so as to photograph them in a way that identifies the principles and laws they embody. The examples in "Elemental Building Forms" are intended to elucidate such design processes and thus to enhance the status of design in architecture. Design of high quality should be a model for us today.

I.

Alt und neu
im Dialog

Anpassung an Vorhandenes

Vom Raum zur Raumdurchdringung

Addierte Elemente der Baugestalt

Old and new
in dialogue

Adaptation to the existing

From space to spatial interpenetration

Added elements of architectural design

1. Anpassung an Vorhandenes

1. Adaptation to the existing

Alte Universität am Rheinsprung Basel (Schweiz)

Einbau von Hörsälen an der zoologischen Anstalt, von Florian Vischer und Georges Weber, Basel, 1959–61.

Das Gebäude mit Bogenarkaden war der älteste Sitz der Baseler Universität am Rheinsprung. Der daneben erstellte zweistöckige Neubau wurde in die maßstäblich kleinteilige Rheinfront eingefügt.

Old university on the Rheinsprung, Basle (Switzerland)

Addition of auditoria to the Department of Zoology by Florian Vischer and Georges Weber, Basle, 1959–61.

The building with open arcading on the Rheinsprung is the oldest building of Basle university. The new two-storey structure adjoining it was matched to the small-scale pattern of the Rhine façade.

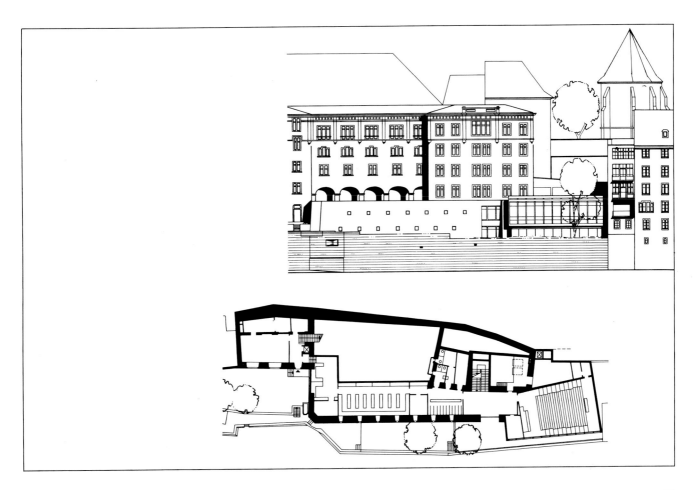

Zentralsparkasse Florisdorf in Wien (Österreich)

Erweiterung der zweiten Filiale Florisdorf „am Spitz", von Friedrich Kurrent und Johannes Spalt, Wien, 1970–74.

Das bestehende markante Gebäude an der Pragerstraße aus der Gründerzeit (1896) wurde äußerlich belassen, innen umgebaut und mit einem neuen Teil auf einem trapezförmigen Grundstück verbunden. Durch Abstufungen des Baukörpers und Jalousien an der Südseite wird das Neue mit dem Alten in Einklang gebracht.

Florisdorf Savings Bank, Vienna (Austria)

Extension of the 2nd branch of the Florisdorf Savings Bank by Friedrich Kurrent and Johannes Spalt, Vienna, 1970–74.

The imposing existing building in the Pragerstrasse dating from the period of promoterism (1896) was not changed externally but the interior was altered and integrated with a new structure built on a trapezoidal site. The new is harmonized with the old by means of gradations in the massing and jalousies on the south side.

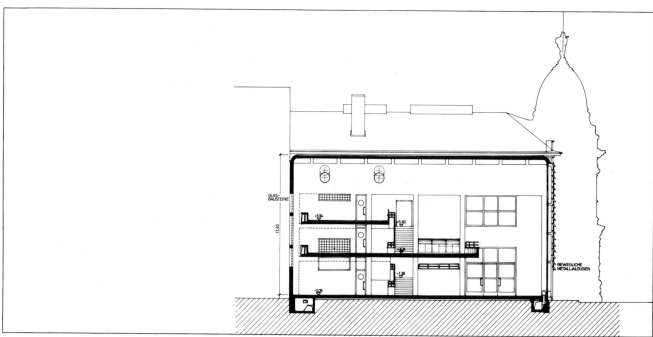

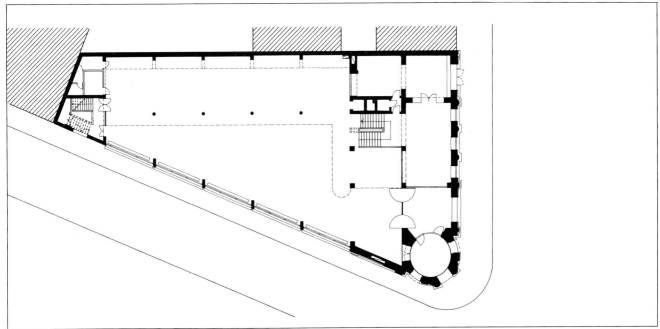

Anbauprojekt Haus Steiner in Küsnacht (Schweiz)

Anbauprojekt eines Gartenpavillons an ein bestehendes Einfamilienhaus (gebaut von Otto Brechbühl 1938–39) in Himmeri, Küßnacht, von Werner Blaser, Basel, 1978–79.

Das abfallende Gelände, markiert von Büschen und Bäumen, mit dem kubischen rationalen Bauwerk war für das Anbauprojekt mitbestimmend. Über die Dachebene zieht sich die Vegetation. Versenkungen in der Bodenebene ergeben Sitz- und Abstellmöglichkeiten. Der Raum bleibt möbelfrei.

Project for adding a pavilion to the Steiner house at Küsnacht (Switzerland)

Project for adding a garden pavilion to an existing private house (built by Otto Brechbühl 1938–39), Himmeri, Küssnacht, by Werner Blaser, Basle, 1978–79.

The sloping site with its bushes and trees and the rationally designed cubic building were among the determinants of the project. The vegetation extends over the roof level. Sunken levels in the floor provide seats and storage surfaces. The room contains no furniture.

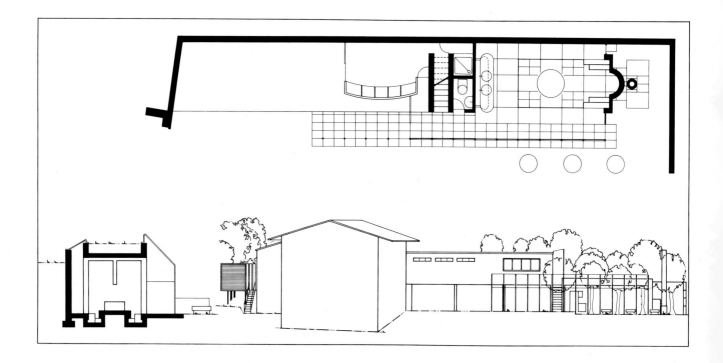

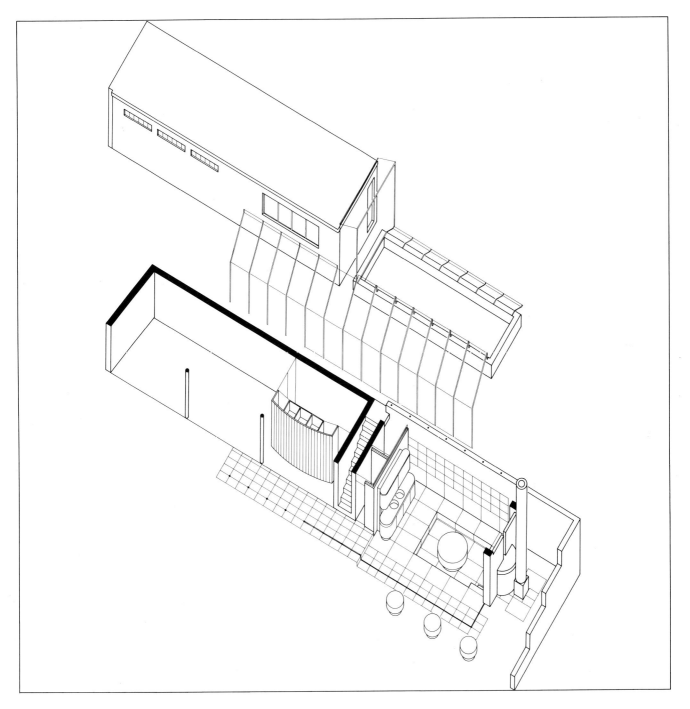

2. Vom Raum zur Raumdurchdringung

2. From space to spatial interpenetration

Piazza Grande in Locarno (Schweiz)

Mobile Raumstrukturen auf der Piazza Grande „Festival internazionale del Film" Locarno, von Livio Vacchini, Locarno, 1972.

Der Boden als bauliche Landschaft, auf dem das Raumfachwerk – der große Bildschirm – zum Nutzen des Menschen und zur Verschönerung seines Lebens beiträgt.

Piazza Grande at Locarno (Switzerland)

Mobile spatial structures on the Piazza Grande "Festival internazionale del Film" Locarno, by Livio Vacchini, Locarno, 1972.

The ground as a structural landscape where the grid structure supporting the giant screen is not only of utility to man but also serves to embellish the world in which he lives.

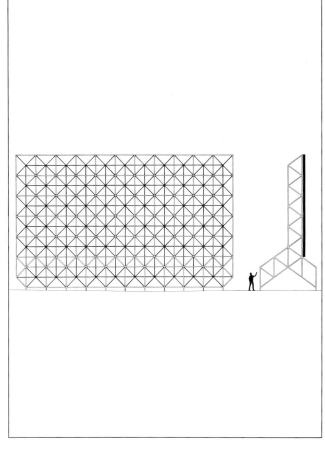

Minnesota Capitol Complex-Projekt (USA)

von C. F. Murphy mit Helmut Jahn, Chicago, 1975.

Die Parklandschaft um das Minnesota-Capitol sollte erhalten bleiben. Ein Einschnitt in die Parkfläche längs zum Capitolgebäude bringt Licht und Luft in das zu bauende Volumen. Das monumentale Gebäude wird durch Neubauten nicht beeinträchtigt.

Minnesota Capitol Complex project (USA)

by C. F. Murphy with Helmut Jahn, Chicago, 1975.

The park-like landscape round the Minnesota Capitol is to be preserved. A cutting into the park area along the Capitol building brings light and air into the volume earmarked for development. New structures will not be allowed to detract from the monumental building.

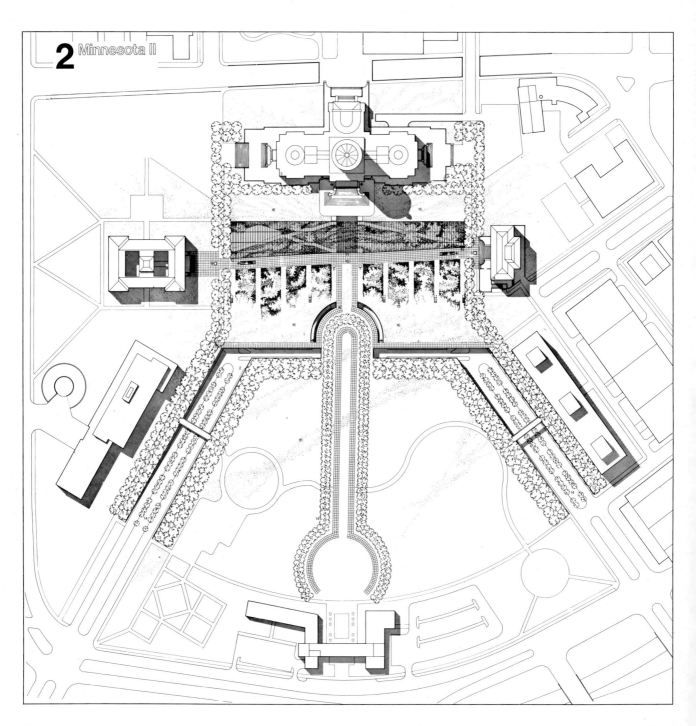

Neugestaltung des Barfüsserplatzes in Basel (Schweiz)

von Werner Blaser, Basel, 1978−80.

Räumliche, architektonische und städtebauliche Funktion eines zentralen Platzes. Konstituierende Elemente waren Boden, Wand, Himmel, Licht, Bäume, Nahtstellen. Die gotische Barfüsserkirche war wichtigstes Element des großen Platzes. Die Pflasterung in 1,20 m großen Rhomben unterstrich die Großzügigkeit des Platzes.

Redesign of the Barfüsserplatz in Basle (Switzerland)

by Werner Blaser, Basle, 1978−80.

The spatial, architectural and urban planning function of a centrally located square. The constitutive elements were ground, wall, sky, light, trees and boundaries. The Gothic Barfüsser Church was of prime importance. The paving in diamonds of 1.20 metres creates a generous impression over the whole area and is particularly suited to the boundaries between the various spaces.

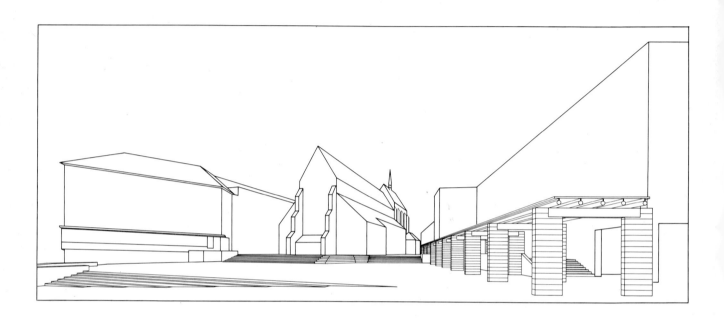

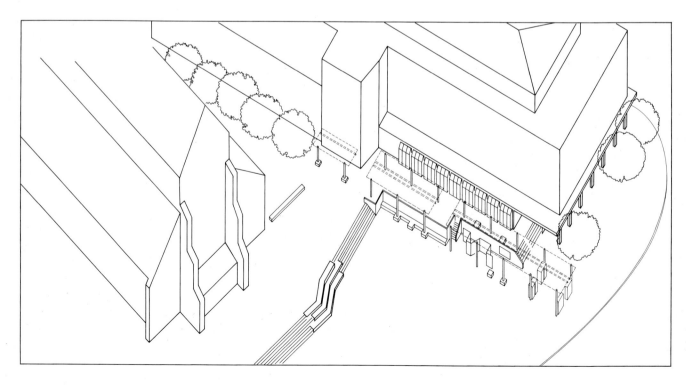

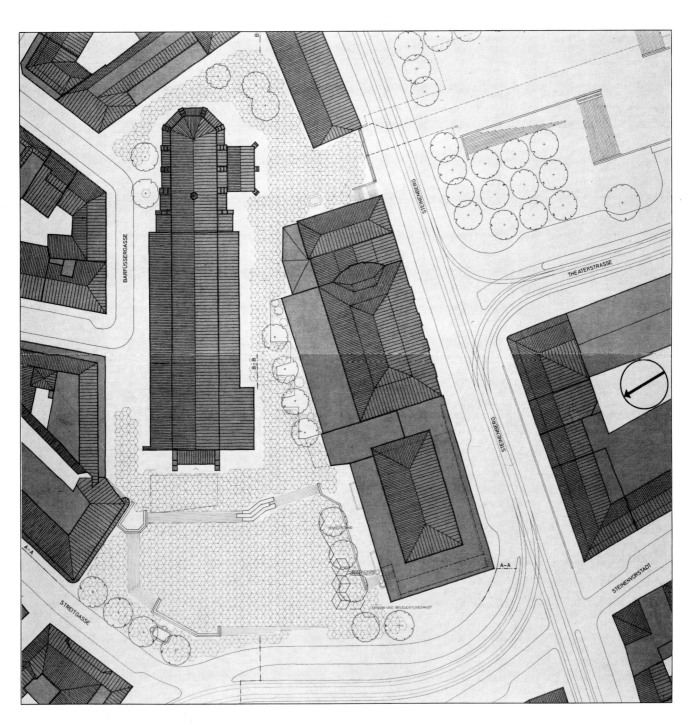

BARFÜSSERGASSE

STREITGASSE

A–A

B–B

B

STEINENBERG

THEATERSTRASSE

STEINENBERG

STEINENVORSTADT

A–A

WANDZEITUNG

FAHNEN- UND BELEUCHTUNGSMAST

21

3. Addierte Elemente der Baugestalt

3. Added elements of architectural design

Fabrikgebäude in Bern (Schweiz)

Ehemalige Textilfabrik, teilweise in ein Architekturbüro umgebaut (Dalmazi, Bern, um 1900).

Um die Jahrhundertwende fand der Mauerziegel als zuverlässiger und wirtschaftlicher Wandbaustoff neue Anwendungsbereiche für die zweckdienliche Gestaltung. Noch heute sind diese Bauwerke aktuell.

Factory building in Berne (Switzerland)

A former textile factory converted into an architect's office and other units (Dalmazi, Berne, c. 1900).

Just at the turn of the century new applications were found for brickwork as a reliable and inexpensive walling material in new and purposive designs. These buildings still have significance for us today.

St. Antoniuskirche in Basel (Schweiz)

Einbindung der St. Antoniuskirche in Basel, von Karl Moser, Zürich, 1926—27.

Die klassische Sichtbeton-Konstruktion zeigt, daß der Beton nicht nur Füllstoff und Tragkörper, sondern auch Dekor sein kann. Die Kirche ist in die Flucht der beidseitig stehenden vier- bis fünfgeschossigen Häuser eingebaut.

Church of St. Antonius in Basle (Switzerland)

Integration of the Church of St. Antonius at Basle by Karl Moser, Zurich, 1926—27.

The classical raw-concrete construction shows that concrete is not only a weight-bearing and infilling material but can also be decorative. The church is integrated in the façade of four- and five-storeyed houses on either side.

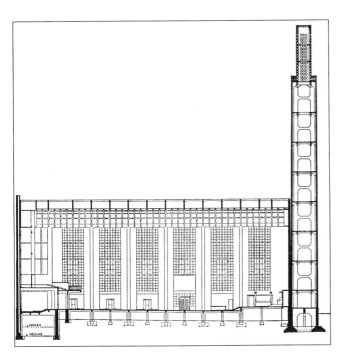

Casa Nascosta in Ascona (Schweiz)

Loggia über zwei Ebenen der Casa Nascosta in Ascona, von Werner Blaser, Basel, 1978–79.

Sanierung eines einfachen Steinhauses mit einer großen Loggia in Holz. Auf der Wohnebene zur Loggia hin wurde die Steinfassade vollständig geöffnet.

Casa Nascosta at Ascona (Switzerland)

Loggia over two levels of the Casa Nascosta at Ascona, by Werner Blaser, Basle, 1978–79.

Redesign of a simple stone house with a large wooden loggia. The stone façade was made completely open towards the loggia at the residential level.

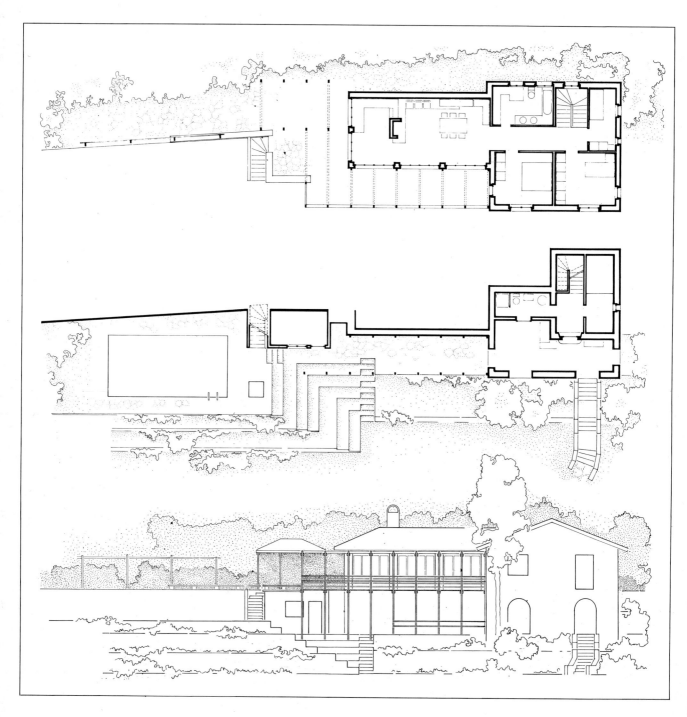

II.

Bewährte Elemente der Architektur

Elementare Architektur
Tradierte Architektur
Expressive Architektur

Proven elements of architecture

Indigenous architecture
Vernacular architecture
Expressive architecture

1. Elementare Architektur

1. Indigenous architecture

Unter elementarer Architektur wird hier eine Architektur von urwüchsigen, erdgebundenen und spontanen Elementen verstanden. In der Geschichte der Architektur wird diese bäuerliche oder einheimische Architektur kaum erwähnt. Im Jahre 1964 setzte sich Bernard Rudofsky aus New York mit der „Architektur ohne Architekten" auseinander. Als Folge dieser Arbeit wurden Architekten und Gestalter auf die Jahrhunderte alte Tradition dieser Form der Architektur und die handwerkliche Geschicklichkeit ihrer Erbauer und Bewohner aufmerksam. Diese zweckmäßigen, mit dem am Ort vorhandenen Baumaterial konstruierten Bauten entsprachen den wirtschaftlichen und sozialen Verhältnissen ihrer Zeit und besitzen heute noch eine augenfällige Übereinstimmung mit der Umwelt. Die mit geringstem Komfort ausgestattete, elementar-einfache Architektur war eins mit der Lebensweise und hat sich in abgelegenen Gebieten über Jahrhunderte bis heute erhalten.

Die Neubesinnung auf die innigste Notwendigkeit – also die Abkehr vom geistlosen Komfort – könnte uns wieder den Weg zu einer neuen Tradition von Leben und Wohnen weisen. Die alten Methoden müßten aber mit den heutigen Mitteln neu interpretiert werden. Die „anonyme" Architektur, wie diese Art von Bauten oft genannt wird, ist durch ihre Erdhaftigkeit klar erkennbar durch eine in unserer Zivilisation verlorengegangene und ihr entgegengesetzte Baugesinnung. In diesem Zusammenhang hat der Professor Peter Dürrenmatt einmal gesagt: „Mehr und mehr Menschen gehen die Augen dafür auf, daß wir die Zeugen eines anderen Zeitgeistes nicht zerstören sollten. Sie machen unser Leben gleichsam wärmer."

Die Grundlage der Konstruktion, das technisch Notwendige und die Frage des Materials sind die Voraussetzungen, die die elementare Architektur unmittelbar und präzise charakterisieren. Elementares Bauschaffen wird somit an drei Merkmalen dargestellt:

☐ Erdnahe und örtliche Bedeutung des Materials

☐ Einfache und handwerklich machbare Konstruktion

☐ Soziale und kulturelle Funktionalität.

By this is meant an architecture of rough elements obtained locally, and constructed in accord with native practice. In the history of architecture there has been little mention of peasant or indigenous architecture. In 1964 Bernard Rudofsky of New York addressed himself to the study of "Architecture without Architects". This work turned the attention of architects and designers to the centuries-old tradition of manual skills displayed by those who erected and lived in such buildings. These buildings, constructed to serve a particular function and using local materials, met economic and social needs and, even today, still display a remarkable unity with their environment. It is an architecture which, constructed with elemental simplicity and rudimentary in its amenities, attained oneness with the life of the people and, in remote regions, has survived to the present day. Careful reflection on this most urgent of our needs – the rejection of materialistic conveniences and amenities – would once again point the way to a new pattern of living and housing.

However, the methods of the past would have to be reinterpreted with the materials and methods of today. This "anonymous" architecture, as such buildings are often and perhaps incorrectly called, is clearly recognizable by its autochthonous quality and by a philosophy of building which has been lost in our present civilization and is opposed to it. In this connection Professor Peter Dürrenmatt once said: "More and more people are opening their eyes to the fact that we should not destroy the monuments left by the genius of another period. It is as if they made our lives warmer."

This indigenous architecture is indelibly and clearly marked by its structural system, by its constructional necessity, and by its materials. It is therefore characterized by three features:

☐ Rough indigenous materials

☐ Unsophisticated methods of construction

☐ Social and economic functionality.

Le Village des Bories in Gordes im Vaucluse (Frankreich)
Architektonische Urform in Stein

Le village des Bories at Gordes in the Vaucluse (France)
Archetypal building form in stone

Der reine Steinbau ist in weit abgelegenen Siedlungen seit etwa dem 18. Jahrhundert beheimatet, wie z. B. in der Provence (Gordes) oder in Apulien, Sardinien, Nordafrika und Nordirland. Diese Gebiete sind heute zweifach bedroht: durch die Abwanderung der Bevölkerung und durch den Ansturm des Massentourismus. Beides führt zu einer Zerstörung der architektonischen Landschaft. Es handelt sich dabei um eine fatale Wechselwirkung: der Besucher kommt aus Freude an der schönen Landschaft und trägt gleichzeitig zu ihrer Zerstörung bei. Man darf die Dinge nicht frei laufen lassen. Die Aufgabe ist die Erhaltung des Ursprünglichen − d. h. nicht nur einzelner Objekte, sondern des ganzen Ortsbildes in seiner einheitlichen Form von Weg − Haus − Raum. Außer durch Sanierungsmaßnahmen kann die urtümliche Steinarchitektur durch eine neue Nutzung vor dem Verfall gerettet werden. Die folgenden Bilder versuchen, das Verständnis um den Einklang von Natur und Bau zu wecken, nicht seiner Altertümlichkeit, sondern seiner würdevollen Schönheit wegen: Vertiefung statt Verflachung, Geborgenheit statt falscher Romantik.

Es gibt Bories, deren Abmessungen noch interessanter sind, die sogar archaisch sein mögen; die Bories im Gebiet von Gordes zeigen fünf Gruppen von Wohnanwesen, die sich um Höfe scharen und fünf Wohneinheiten mit ihren Nebengehöften bilden. Die Bories sind nach dem Prinzip des falschen, aus Kragsteinen gebildeten Gewölbes gebaut; die Steine wurden trocken aufeinandergeschichtet.

Since the 18th century, the use of stone alone for building is to be seen in remote settlements like those in Provence (Gordes), or in Apulia, Sardinia, North Africa and Ireland. These areas have again become battlefields in which depopulation is waging a struggle against the onslaught of mass tourism. The result has been the destruction of the architectural landscape. What we have here is an unfortunate interaction: the visitor comes because he takes pleasure in the beautiful landscape and at the same time he helps to destroy it. We must not let him do as he pleases. It is our task to preserve what is original and native with regard not only to single objects but also to the whole pattern of the place in the oneness of its streets, houses and space. Apart from measures of renewal, this indigenous stone architecture can be preserved from destruction by being put to new uses. The collection of photographs attempts to instil appreciation of the harmony of nature and buildings not out of antiquarian considerations but because of their inherent dignity and beauty: delving below the surface rather than being content with superficialities; seeking a sense of security rather than cultivating false romanticism.

There are Bories which are on a larger scale and may even be of archaic origin. The Bories in the region of Gordes show five groups of homesteads huddled round courtyards and forming five dwelling units together with their outbuildings. The Bories are built on the principle of a corbelled vault, the stones being set in projecting courses.

Das Raumfachwerk als Einheit in Decke und Hülle zeigt Bezüge zu den Kuppelbauten aus Stein, in denen Material und Konstruktion eins sind.

Lagerhalle J. Lüber in Märkt, Deutschland. Werner Blaser, Basel, 1969–70.

The grid structure as a unit in the floor and protective envelope has affinities with stone dome structures where material and construction are one.

Warehouse J. Lüber at Märkt, Germany, Werner Blaser, Basle, 1969–1970.

Gesamtplan der Wohnsiedlung im Freilichtmuseum in Gordes.

General plan of the village settlement in the Open-Air Museum at Gordes.

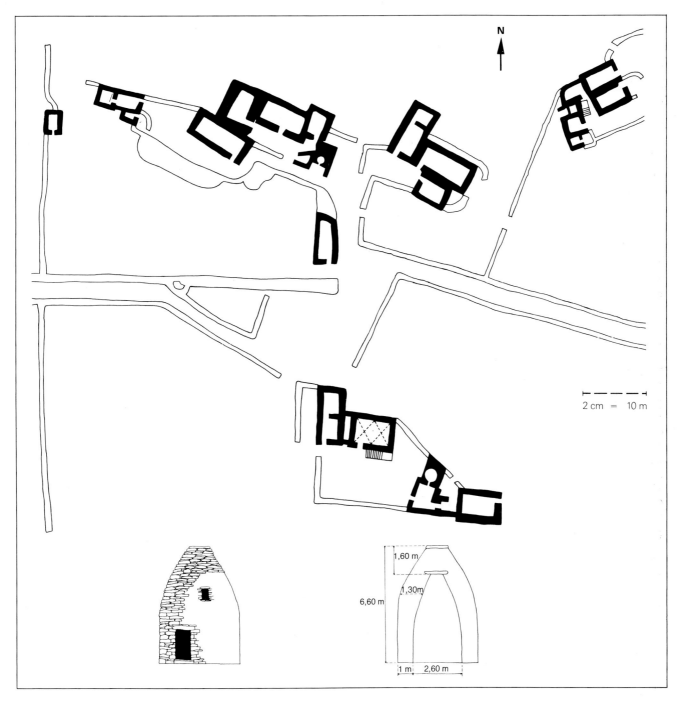

N

2 cm = 10 m

1,60 m

1,30m

6,60 m

1 m   2,60 m

Provenzialische Steinhütten der „Bories". Die Anlage in Gordes ist etwa 200 Jahre alt; das Prinzip der Kuppelbauten ist seit mindestens 3000 Jahren bekannt.

Provençal stone huts of the "Bories". The site at Gordes is said to be 200 years old; the principle of cupola building has been known for at least 3000 years.

Steine werden trocken geschichtet und nach außen geneigt, um das Eindringen von Wasser zu verhindern.

The stones are arranged in courses without mortar and inclined outward in order to make the walls watertight.

Kragsteinbauten sind von Höfen umschlossen. Corbelled structures are surrounded by courtyards.

Kragsteinbau: Innenschale bienenkorbförmig, Außenschale als Spitzpyramide.

Corbelled structure: the inner shell is like a beehive in shape, the external envelope is a pointed pyramid.

Rundhütte, eine urtümliche stabile Bauform, Ende des 17. oder Anfang des 18. Jahrhunderts gebaut.

Circular hut, a stable type of indigenous structure built in the late 17th or early 18th century.

Kragkuppel: Ein Minimum an Material – ein Maximum an Volumen.

Corbelled cupola: a minimum of material – a maximum of volume.

Steinbauten ohne Mörtel errichtet, innen mit grobem Mörtel verputzt, der Wind und Insekten am Eindringen hindert.

Drystone structures, rendered inside with coarse mortar to keep out wind and insects.

Die Häuser sind innen vielfach zweistöckig ausgeführt oder besitzen in der Wärmezone des Kaminfeuers ein überhöhtes halbes Stockwerk.

Inside there are often two storeys or a raised half storey in the zone of warmth round the fireplace.

Bauformen auf Irland und den Aran-Inseln im Atlantik

Die Bilder stellen den Versuch dar, ein Material und seine Verwendung in den elementarsten Grundlagen zu schildern, damit beginnend, wie Stein auf Stein gelegt wird. Die Wahl beschränkt sich hier auf Irland und auf eine kleine Insel im Atlantik vor Galway, die Aran-Insel Inisheer.

Auf dieser Insel fehlt es an Vegetation durch den Mangel an Humus: es gibt nur Stein als Baumaterial, zum Teil von Natur aus in Blockform, so daß er ohne weiteres aufeinandergeschichtet werden kann. Dieser einfachsten konstruktiven Ordnung gehen die Bilder nach. Die primitive heimische Steinarchitektur kommt zu einer Belebung unseres heutigen Bauschaffens gerade zur richtigen Zeit. Dabei geht es um die Erhaltung und Aufwertung von Sachwerten, aber nicht nur in rein denkmalschützerischer Absicht, sondern auch zur Konservierung von mauerumschlossenen Gehegen.

Für die Steinwälle auf der Aran-Insel Inisheer ist für den Tourismus ein Umfunktionieren nicht möglich; sie dienen nur den Haustieren als Unterkunft. Überall bildet der Stein die Grundlage allen Bauens: von der herben Ursprünglichkeit der Mauern und Kuppelbauten, den noch vorhandenen keltischen High-Cross, bis zu den weiß gekalkten Strohdachhütten. Ohne Stein und das mit ihm Geschaffene ist kein Haus möglich.

Building forms in Ireland and on the Aran Isles in the Atlantic

The photographs are an attempt to show a material and the way it is used in its most basic form, beginning with one stone laid on another. The choice of examples is limited to Ireland and a small island in the Atlantic, Inisheer, one of the Aran Islands off Galway.

On this island the absence of humus has prevented the growth of vegetation: the only building material available is stone, partly in the form of natural blocks which can be laid in courses one on top of the other without further treatment. I made a study of this most simple system of construction. This indigenous stone architecture, which has survived the passage of centuries to be rediscovered today, comes as a most timely aid to us in breathing new life into our present-day building. What is involved here is the preservation and upgrading of tangible assets, with a view not merely to protecting buildings as historical monuments but also to conserving stone-walled enclosures.

In the case of the walled enclosures of the Aran Islands, a change of function to serve the purposes of tourism, as has happened in Switzerland, is not practical politics for they serve simply as accommodation for the beasts. Everywhere stone is the basic all-purpose building material: from the walls and beehive huts with their rough, autochthonous quality and the still extant Celtic High Cross to the whitewashed thatched cottages. Without stone and things made of stone, house dwelling is impossible.

Die Mauer im urbanen Hofhaus als Umschließung. Begrenzung und Öffnung ist das Grundprinzip einer altüberlieferten Wohnform und bleibt ein Beispiel von gestern und heute.

Haus mit drei Höfen, Projekt L. Mies van der Rohe, Berlin, 1934.

The wall as enclosure in the town courtyard house. ▷ This traditional old type of house embodies the basic principle of closure and opening and remains an example from yesterday still valid today.

House with three courtyards, project L. Mies van der Rohe, Berlin, 1934.

Aran-Insel „Inisheer", eine steinige und fast vege-
tationslose Gegend. Die Insel ist der irischen Küste
im Westen der Galway-Bay vorgelagert.

Inisheer, stony and almost devoid of vegetation, is
one of the Aran Islands off the Irish coast to the
west of Galway Bay.

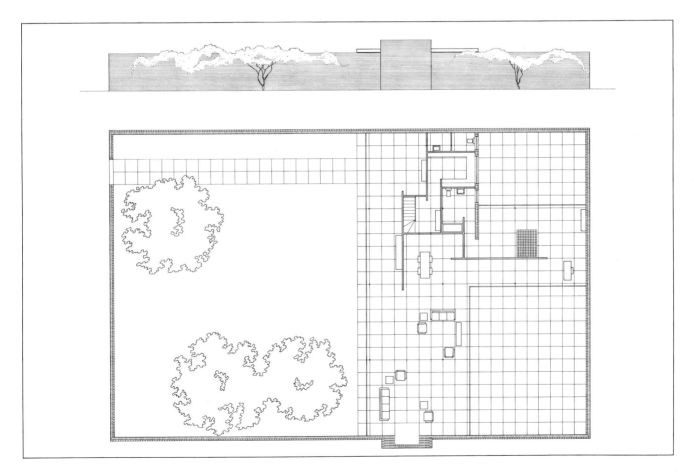

Steine – ungeformt und geformt in der gewachse-
nen Landschaft.

Stones, shaped and unshaped, figure in the organic
pattern of the landscape.

Steingehege für die Behausung der Tiere.

Stone enclosure in which to pen cattle.

Der Not gehorchend, spannt der irische Inselbe-
wohner mit den Steinmauern für Behausung und
Gehege ein Rasternetz über die ganze Insel.

Necessity obliges the Irish island farmer to cast over
the whole island a network of walls forming enclosures for housing and for stock-raising.

Hütte auf der irischen Atlantikinsel, aus unbehaue-
nen Steinen errichtet und aus der Umfassungsmau-
er entwickelt.

Hut of undressed field stones evolved out of the
enclosing wall on the Irish isle in the Atlantic.

Aufeinandergeschichtete Wälle überziehen das flache Land.

Drystone walls run over the flat land.

Primitive Steinbauten aus Mauern ohne Mörtel und Dächern mit Riedgras. Haus und Landschaft sind eins.

Primitive drystone structures, roofs with reed thatching. The house and the landscape are unified.

Bauernhäuser auf dem Festland in Donegal, weiß-gekälkt und strohgedeckt. Das einzige verfügbare Baumaterial bildet Haus- und Begrenzungsmauern.

Farmhouses on the mainland in Donegal, lime-washed and thatched with straw. The only material available forms the walls of the house and enclosures.

Walser-Häuser aus Alagna Valsesia (Italien)
Holz als Träger und als Ausfachung

Walser houses from Alagna Valsesia (Italy)
Wood as weight-bearer — wood as infilling

Das Bauprinzip, das wir heutzutage mit dem Ausdruck „Skin und Skeleton" (Haut und Knochen) zu bezeichnen pflegen, ist uralt. Denken wir nur an den griechischen Tempelbau. Die klare Ordnung von Säule und Architrav, von Träger und Last, wird deutlich sichtbar. Auch bei den elementaren Bauten im südlichen Alpengebiet finden wir die sinnvolle Anwendung des Skelettbaus, wo nur Fels und Wald das Baumaterial liefern. Beim Maiensäss oder bei den Alphütten der Bergkolonisten der Walser, die ursprünglich aus dem benachbarten Wallis kamen, sind Fundamente und zum Teil Eckpfeiler aus Stein, die Ausfachung und das Dachgebälk aus Holz.

Die objektive Struktur der Statik steht in Spannung zur subjektiven Gestalt. Einfacher geht es nicht mehr: Fundamente und Wandelemente sind solide aufgebaut, Ausfachung und Dach spielerisch gestaltet. Im Skelettprinzip wird darum klar unterschieden zwischen der Struktur als Gefüge und Aufbau und der Textur als Oberfläche und Wirkung. Die von mehreren Seiten umschließenden Terrassen zum Trocknen und Aufhängen von Erntegut prägen mit der horizontalen Gliederung den Baustil der Walser Stadel. Das sonnenverbrannte Lärchenholz und die mit Granitplatten bedeckten Dächer verbinden sich zu einheitlichen Siedlungstypen und Bildern.

The system of structure we today call "skin and skeleton" is no invention of the 20th century but goes back to ancient times. The Greek temple immediately springs to mind. There the system of pillar and architrave, "load and load-bearer", is clearly visible. Again in the indigenous buildings of the southern area of the Alps we find that highly efficient use has been made of the skeleton structure in places where the rock and the forest alone supply the materials. In the shielings on the alpine pastures and the alpine huts built by the Walsers, who migrated from the neighbouring Valais and, colonizing certain mountain areas, established a settlement at Alagna, the plinths and to some extent the corner pillars are of stone while the infilling and the roof beams are of wood.

The statics of the structure are objective and contrast strongly with the subjectively conceived dynamics: the plinths and the wall elements are of solid construction whereas the infills and the roof are designed with a lighter touch. In the skeleton building the structure as the supporting system is therefore clearly distinguished from the envelope surface and ornamentation. Terraces arranged on more than one side of the building and serving to dry crops emphasize the horizontal lines of the Walser barn. The sunburnt larch wood and the roofs weighed down with granite slabs combine to unify the view of the village as a whole as well as its individual aspects.

Darstellung eines zweistöckigen Blockspeichers aus dem Museo Walser in Alagna, ein Dorf mit charakteristischem Siedlungsbild der Walser.

Representation of a two-storey log-built barn from ▷ the Walser Museum at Alagna, a village showing the characteristic layout adopted by the Walsers.

Dachelement und Frontfassade aus Holz sind in die Steinstruktur eingeschoben nach dem Prinzip von Skelett und Ausfachung oder Gerüst und Haut.

Ferienhaus am Meer in Les Mathes (Frankreich) von Le Corbusier und P. Jeanneret, Paris, 1935.

Roof element and front façade executed in wood and inserted into the stone structure on the principle of framework and infill or skin and skeleton.

Seaside holiday house, Les Mathes (France), Le Corbusier and P. Jeanneret, Paris, 1935.

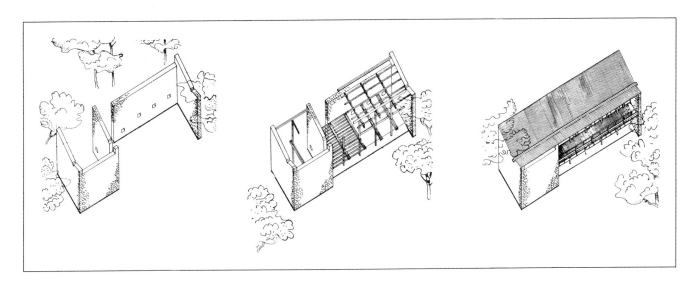

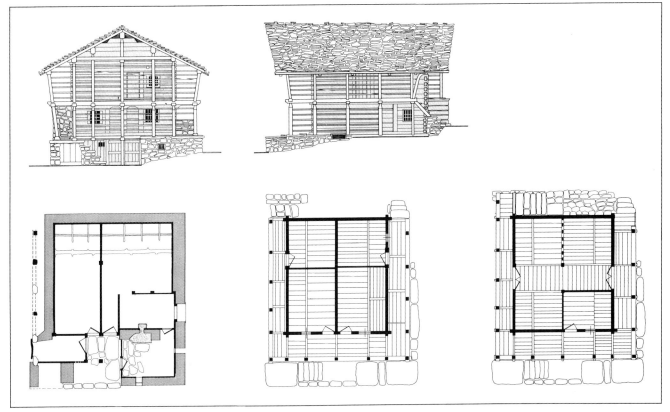

Blockstadel mit schräg auskragendem Laubengang. Die Laube ist durch ein Riegelgitter geschlossen.

Stone-built barn with obliquely cantilevered gallery. The gallery is enclosed by a wooden lattice.

Dreiseitige Umgangslauben mit ausladenden Trok-
kengestellen aus Riegeln an Stäben und Bohlen.

Gallery round three sides with cantilevered drying
frames with nogging pieces, studs and planks.

Das Walsermuseum in Alagna (1191 m.ü.M.) liegt zuoberst im Sesia-Tal über Varallo unterhalb des Monte Rosa.

The Walser Museum at Alagna (1191 m) is located at the head of the Valle della Sesia above Varallo at the foot of Monte Rosa.

Wie ein filigranes Netz umschließen horizontale Stäbe die Umgangslauben.

Horizontal bars enclose the galleries like a filigree.

Die Ständerlaube ist vor den Blockbau gestellt.

The gallery is arranged in front of the log construction.

Alpi d'Otro über Alagna (1674 m.ü.M.). Blockbau und Holzstäbe sind durch die Sonne braungebrannt und verleihen dem Bauwerk zusammen mit dem linearen Fassadenbild ein einheitliches Gepräge.

Alpi d'Otro (1674 m) above Alagna. The log construction and the wooden studs are burnt brown by the sun and, together with the linear pattern of the façade, confer unity on the building.

Hinter dem Monte Rosa liegen in einheitlicher Gestalt die Maiensässe, dazu das einheitliche Material: Granit und dunkelgebranntes Holz.

The alpine shielings behind Monte Rosa display a unity of design which is further emphasized by the unity of materials: granite and wood burnt dark by the sun.

2. Tradierte Architektur

Eine Architektur aus traditionellen einheimischen und bäuerlichen Elementen paßt zu den kulturellen Verhältnissen einer Landschaft und weist auf geschickte Verwendung des vorhandenen Baumaterials hin. Gerade heute wieder beschäftigt den Architekten naturbewußtes, landschaftsgebundenes Bauen. Stein ist das natürliche Material, das erdgebundenes Bauen von jeher formte und charakterisierte. Die moderne Architektur hat Stein auf verschiedene Weise verwendet: vom übertünchten Naturstein bis zu Gebilden mit Blocksteinen. Zum Beispiel entwickelte der spätere Le Corbusier (1887–1965) eine expressive Architektur des „Béton brut" oder Ludwig Mies von der Rohe (1888–1969) stellte Stein den technischen Materialien Stahl und Glas gegenüber.

Wenn der Stadtbewohner Haus sagt, denkt er unwillkürlich und in erster Linie an das Äußere, die Fassade. Bei der geschlossenen Gesellschaft der Landbevölkerung aber steht an erster Stelle das Innere des Hauses, der Innenraum – hier durch Planzeichnungen dargestellt.

Aus dem Wirken und Leben der Benutzer entstand somit die architektonische Gestalt. Nach einem Zitat Fritz Schumachers von 1926 (Städteplaner aus Hamburg 1869–1947) gibt es überhaupt keine Architektur ohne Auseinandersetzung mit einem Stück Welt und einem Stück Menschenbedürfnis.

Die Möglichkeiten einer Architektur, die auf diesen Prinzipien beruhen, sind die Integration von Mensch und Natur, von Konstruktion und Gestalt, von Innenraum und Außenraum. In der Eigenart dieser Beziehungen liegt es, daß Struktur und Gestalt nicht in momentaner Perfektion erstarren, sondern zwischen den Gesetzmäßigkeiten der einzelnen Beziehungspunkte hin und her pendeln.

Drei wesentliche Momente bestimmen die tradierte Architektur:

☐ Spezifische Eigenheiten der Landschaft und ihre geschichtliche Entwicklung

☐ Traditionelle Bauformen als konstruktive Lösung grundlegender Bedürfnisse

☐ Anpassungsfähigkeit und Nutzungsneutralität außen und innen.

2. Vernacular architecture

An architecture of traditional local and rural elements, wisely used, matches the cultural aspects of a landscape and shows how the building material available can be skilfully utilized. Perhaps more than ever before, the architect of today is exercised by the problem of building in conformity with nature and the landscape. Stone is the natural material which has shaped and characterized the earth from time immemorial. Modern architects have used stone in various ways from whitewashed natural stone to structures of building blocks. For example, in his later works Le Corbusier (1887–1965) developed an expressive architecture of "béton brut" and Ludwig Mies van der Rohe (1886–1969) contrasted stone with the industrial products steel and glass.

When the town dweller says "house", he thinks first and foremost of the external appearance, the façade. In the closed community of the rural population on the other hand it is the inside of the house, the interior, represented here by plans, which is uppermost.

It was out of the work and the life of the people using the house that the architectural form was derived. In 1926 Fritz Schumacher (town planner from Hamburg, 1869–1947) said that there is no architecture of any kind without a confrontation with a "piece of the world and a piece of human need".

An architecture resting on these principles makes it possible to integrate man and nature as well as construction and form both in the interior and on the outside. The special nature of this relationship explains why structure and form do not congeal in monumental perfection but can be modulated between reference points at which ordered systems prevail.

Three essential factors determine vernacular architecture:

☐ Specific characteristics of the landscape and its historical development

☐ Traditional structural forms as the constructional answer to basic requirements

☐ Adaptability and diversity of use inside and outside.

Blockbauten aus der Region Maramures (Rumänien)
Tektonisches Prinzip als Grundform

Die folgende Dokumentation von Blockbauten aus Osteuropa verfolgt den Zweck, eine traditionelle Volksarchitektur für unsere Zeit wieder zu erschließen.

Der Tourismus muß sich heute, seiner Eigendynamik folgend, immer wieder neue Gebiete eröffnen und sucht auch das Volksleben miteinzubeziehen. Die wertvollsten kunsthistorischen Werke sind uns bekannt. Aber ist das ausreichend? Führen sie wirklich zum Sehen und Erleben? Gibt es nicht auch wichtige Bereiche, die uns noch nicht zu Bewußtsein gekommen sind? Gerade in Osteuropa findet man immer noch unentdeckte Kostbarkeiten lebendigen Volksgutes. Leben und Bauen sind hier oft noch im Gleichgewicht. Wir finden faszinierende Beispiele der Holzarchitektur, die heute noch genutzt werden.

Tore, Balken und Säulen der Häuser in Rumänien zum Beispiel lassen uns an die Werke des großen Brâncuşi (1876−1957) denken, der von hier, aus der Mitte der Holzschnitzer heraus, nach Paris zog und der modernen Bildhauerkunst entscheidende Impulse gab. Er übertrug die Tradition der bäuerlichen Holzbaukunst in die heutige Zeit − ein Pendant etwa zu Béla Bartók (1881−1945), dessen Musik in der ungarischen Folklore wurzelt. Eine glückliche Darstellung unverfälschter Tradition architektonischer Formen ist im Dorfmuseum in Bukarest inmitten eines Parkes von zehn Hektar Größe zu finden.

Die Region Maramures im Norden des Landes ist heute noch ein Beispiel einer intakten Kultur ihrer Bewohner mit ihrer hervorragenden tektonischen Holzarchitektur, den heute noch lebendig erhaltenen orthodoxen Holzkirchen des 17. und 18. Jahrhunderts und den Bauernhäusern im Blockbausystem, die von geflochtenen Zäunen und prächtig geschmückten Toren umrahmt sind.

Dieses Beispiel bietet weiten Kreisen und besonders auch der jungen Generation eine vorzügliche Möglichkeit, sich zu orientieren und vor der Übernahme bestimmter Stilelemente unserer Zeit eigene Standpunkte zu finden. Dabei ist es erstaunlich, wie viele Möglichkeiten und Variationen einer geistigen Bemühung wert sind.

Log constructions from the region of Maramureş (Rumania)
Architectonic principle as basic form

The documentation from Eastern Europe serves only one purpose, and that is to make traditional vernacular architecture available to our own age. Today tourism must follow its own inherent dynamics and go on opening up new areas for development, seeking at the same time to make the life of the indigenous people part of the visitor's experience. Guidebooks of art history are valuable and familiar enough. But are they sufficient? Are they really a guide to seeing and experiencing? Are there not areas here which are still closed to our inner awareness? It is in Eastern Europe more than anywhere else that we find undiscovered gems of a still vital popular heritage. Everywhere here living and building are still in equilibrium. We find fascinating examples of timber architecture still being used today.

The gateways, beams and pillars of houses in Rumania, for example, recall the works of the great Brancusi (1876−1957), who left the world of woodcarvers to go to Paris and who gave fresh impetus to modern sculpture, embodying the tradition of wooden vernacular architecture in a modern form, just as Bela Bartok (1881−1945) did with his music that is rooted in Hungarian folklore. In the Museum of the Village in Bucharest, set amidst a park of 25 acres, there is a fine display of traditional architecture which is quite genuine and unspoiled.

The region of Maramureş in the north of the country still remains an example of an intact popular culture with its outstanding timber architecture, its Orthodox churches of the 17th and 18th centuries which have survived as living entities until today, and its log-built farmhouses surrounded by wickerwork fences and splendidly ornate gateways.

This example affords a wide public, and particularly the younger generation, an excellent opportunity to appraise its position and decide where its stand is with regard to the design of our own times. It is quite astonishing how many possibilities and variations there are which are worth the mental effort of further examination.

Gewachsenes und Gestaltetes, Ungeformtes und Geformtes können einander zugeordnet sein und zu Elementen der qualitativen Gestaltung führen.

Gästehaus in Bristol, Wisconsin, USA, Alfred Caldwell, seit 1974 im Bau.

Natural growth and design, the amorphous and the shaped, can be correlated to yield elements of qualitative design.

Guesthouse at Bristol, Wisconsin, USA, Alfred Caldwell, under construction since 1974.

Darstellung eines typischen Wohnhauses aus der Region Maramures.

Representation of a typical house from the Maramureş region.

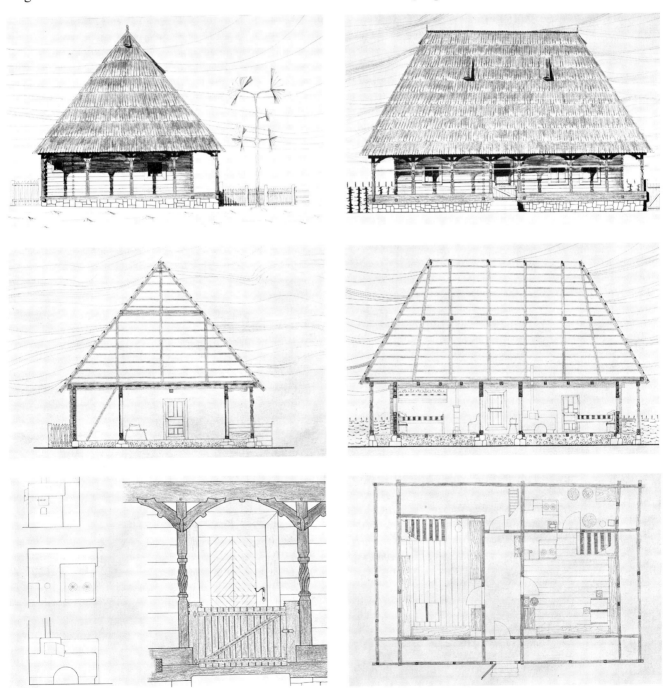

Talkirche von Jeud im Izatal, 1718.   Valley church of Jeud in the Iza valley, 1718.

Bergkirche von Jeud im Izatal, 1364, älteste rumänische orthodoxe Holzkirche.

Mountain church of Jeud in the Iza valley 1364, oldest Rumanian Orthodox timber church.

Wände eines Blockhauses aus horizontal gelegten Balken, Öffnungen für Fenster und Türen werden aus der Wand geschlagen. Als Werkzeug wurde vornehmlich die Axt verwendet.

Log walls of horizontally arranged baulks; openings for windows and doors are trimmed out of the wall. The axe is the chief implement employed.

Bauernhaus aus Budesti im Cosâutal. Die Standfe-stigkeit wird durch die ausgewogene Beziehung von Plattform und Dach demonstriert. Das Bild zeigt die optische freie Zone der Fassade.

Farmhouse from Budeşti in the Cosău valley. Optimally related to the roof, the platform ensures stability. The visually open part of the façade is to be seen here.

Lange schmale Wirtschaftsflächen hinter dem Wohngebäude.

Die grobe Oberflächentextur des Blockhauses, die überblatteten Ecken und die überkragenden Dächer schaffen eine Skulptur.

Long, narrow swathes of farmland behind the house. The rough texture of the logs, the halved corner joints and the jutting roofs create a sculptural quality.

Die Addition der vertikalen Stützen bringt Rhythmus in die klar gegliederte Fassade.

Rhythm is imparted to the clear pattern of the façade by the additive principle of the regularly arranged supports.

Holzkirche von Rozavlea, 1718. Dach und Turm mit Schindeln bekleidet.

Timber church of Rozavlea, 1718. Roof and tower clad with shingles.

Mediterrane Architektur auf Stromboli (Italien)
Element und Masse

In der Architektur stehen seit jeher zwei Grundkonzepte einander gegenüber: die plastisch geformte Höhle und das konstruktiv gliedernde Zelt. Den zeltartigen Charakter im Bauen, bei dem feingliedrige Stäbe über die Fassaden gezogen werden, finden wir hauptsächlich in der Architektur Ostasiens. Die mediterranen Wohnbauten sind dagegen mit der massiven Gestalt der Höhle vergleichbar. Die Höhle ist räumlich gebunden, bei ihrer Bildung wird die Masse verdrängt. Ihrem Wesen entspricht die heutige organische Betonarchitektur. Auf der Insel Stromboli ist die Synthese von objektiv massiger Baustruktur und subjektiv schweifender Landschaftsdarstellung besonders gut gelungen. Die Reihe der dargestellten Bilder soll gipfeln in der Schilderung des räumlichen Spiels der Baukuben und der organischen Fläche der Fassaden.

Le Corbusiers Kapelle in Ronchamp (1950−54) erinnert verblüffend an das gekurvte Wohnhaus auf der Insel Stromboli. Die weiß getünchten Wohnhäuser mit kubischen Formen Strombolis, eine der liparischen Inseln mit tätigen Vulkanen im Mittelmeer, heben sich von der wuchernden südlichen Landschaft ab, bilden aber mit ihren Loggias eine beziehungsvolle Synthese zwischen Außen- und Innenraum.

Leben und Wohnen im Vergänglichen − eine Alternative zu uns.

Mediterranean architecture on Stromboli (Italy)
Element and mass

There have always been two opposed conceptions in architecture: the sculpturally formed cave and the structurally articulated tent. Buildings of this tent-like character, in which the façades are traversed by slender timbers, are to be found mainly in the architecture of East Asia. In contrast, the dwellings of the Mediterranean region are comparable to the massive shape of caves. The cave is space-bound; mass must be displaced to create it. Its character is reflected in the organic concrete architecture of today. On the island of Stromboli a synthesis between the structure of buildings, objectively solid and massive, and the landscape, felt subjectively to be a pattern of curves, has been achieved with particular success. The illustrations shown here culminate in a portrayal of the spatial interplay of the cubes of buildings and the organic surfaces of the façades.

Le Corbusier's chapel at Ronchamp (1950−54) is strikingly reminiscent of the curved dwelling house on the island of Stromboli. The whitewashed cube-shaped dwellings of Stromboli, one of the volcanically active Lipari islands in the Mediterranean Sea, stand out from the luxuriant southern landscape while their loggias create a richly related synthesis between interior and exterior.

Living and homes in the flux of time − an alternative. ▷

Komplexe Beziehungen zur Vergangenheit. Ein Versuch, in der Architektur mediterrane Qualitäten und plastische Tendenzen in neue Zusammenhänge zu bringen. Identifizierung von Mensch und Raum.

Wallfahrtskapelle in Ronchamp, Frankreich, von Le Corbusier, Paris, 1950−1954.

Complex relationship with the past. An attempt in vernacular architecture to establish new relations between Mediterranean quality and sculptural tendencies. Identification of man and space.

Chapel of pilgrimage at Ronchamp, France, by Le Corbusier, Paris, 1950−54.

Kontrast zwischen der üppigen Vegetation und strengen Baukörpern.

Contrast between luxuriant vegetation and severe architecture.

Geometrisches Muster der Rebkulturen auf der Insel.   Geometrical pattern of vineyards on the island.

Isola Stromboli im Tyrrhenischen Meer mit kubischen Bauformen in weißem Putz im Kontrast zu der unter südlicher Sonne vergilbten Vegetation.

Isola Stromboli in the Tyrrhenian Sea with white-plastered cube-shaped buildings contrasting with the vegetation that has turned to the colour of ochre under the southern sun.

Voluminöse, in sich geschlossene Architektur mit spielerischem Einpassen der Loggia.

Voluminous self-contained architecture to which the loggia has been added almost as an afterthought.

Offener Herd mit Gewölbtonnenkonstruktion, Sichtbarmachung der funktionalen Bedingungen.

Open fireplace with barrel vault construction; the functional conditions are expressed.

Plastizität im zweigeschossigen Baukörper – wir denken an Le Corbusiers Wallfahrtskirche in Ronchamp.

Sculptural quality in a two-storey mass – we are reminded of Le Corbusier's chapel of pilgrimage at Ronchamp.

Das Grün der Landschaft in Kontrast zum Weiß der kubischen Urformen sowie die Phantasie der Baumeister in den Mitteln, mit denen die Architektur in Übereinstimmung mit den Gegebenheiten des Terrains gebracht wird, sind die charakteristischen Eigenschaften des Inseldorfes.

The contrast between the green of the landscape and the white of the archetypal cubes together with the imagination displayed in the way the architecture is harmonized with the terrain form the characteristics of the island village.

Bauernhäuser im Burgenland (Österreich)
Haus im mauerumschlossenen Hof

Farmhouses in Burgenland (Austria)
The house in a walled courtyard

Eine der wesentlichsten Erscheinungen einer Kultur ist die Architektur. Es soll nun der Versuch gemacht werden, Prinzipien der struktiven Architektur als Hauptanliegen jedes Bauwerks herauszukristallisieren und das konstruktive Gefüge in Teile zu zerlegen. Die Trennung von Struktur und Dekor läßt das Bauwerk tiefer erkennen.

Es gibt Bauten, die ohne Architekt entstanden sind, die sozusagen aus der Natur herausgewachsen im Raum stehen. Es sind oft Massivbauten, gleichsam nach außen gestülpte Höhlen, ohne Anwendung von einheitlichen Bauprinzipien errichtet. Das reizvolle Gegeneinander und das Zusammenspiel von objektiver Gestaltung und künstlerischer Phantasie sollen hier bildlich dargestellt werden. Ausgewählt wurden dafür Bauernhäuser im Burgenland. Charakteristisch für die Gehöfte im Nordburgenland ist ihre Erdgebundenheit in der plastischen und farbigen Gestaltung. Das Flächendekor läßt der Phantasie und Imagination ungehemmte Freiheit, auch bei klarer Bindung an die Struktur.

One of the most characteristic aspects of a civilization is its architecture. An attempt should now be made to extract the principles of structural architecture as one of the main concerns of every true building and to analyse the composition of building material and elements. It is only when structure is divorced from decoration that a building displays its overall form.

There are buildings which have taken shape without an architect, grown into space, as it were, out of nature; massive constructions like caves turned inside out to which no unified building principles have been applied. The charming interplay of objective design and artistic imagination, now opposed and now conspiring, should be portrayed so as to bring out their essential quality. What is typical of the farmsteads of north Burgenland is the way in which they are bound to the earth by the forms and colours of their design. The surface decoration gives free play to the imagination and fantasy even though it is clearly linked to the structure.

Rurales Bauen im Nordburgenland; osteuropäisch anmutende weite Ebenen und karge Vegetation am Neusiedler See.

Rural building in north Burgenland where ▷ the broad plains and the sparse vegetation on the Neusiedlersee already hint at Eastern Europe.

Verbindung vom Organischen zum Geometrischen; urtümliche plastische Gestaltungskraft in phantasievolle, menschliche Behausungen umgesetzt.

Pueblo-Siedlung in Canyon (USA), etwa 16. Jh. „Built for the people, of the people, by the people".

The organic and the geometric are unified as primal creative power is converted into imaginative human housing.

Pueblo settlement at Canyon, USA, c. 16th century."Built for the people, of the people, by the people."

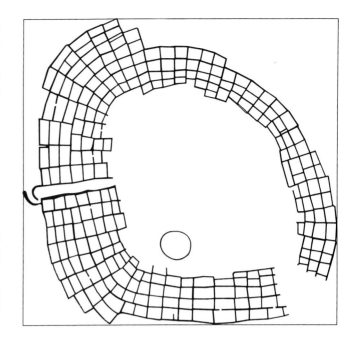

Darstellung der Giebel und Eingangstore gegen die Hauptstraße von Trausdorf.

Gables and entrance gates fronting on the high street of Trausdorf.

Hofhäuser hinter schützenden Mauern in Oslip (Kroatien).

Courtyard houses behind protective walls at Oslip (Croatia).

Reihung gleichartiger Häusertypen mit barocker Giebelfassade; Fensterläden in Metall und grün gemalter Einfassung.

Array of identical house types with Baroque gabled façades; shutters of metal in greenpainted surrounds.

St. Margarethen, Geborgenheit in mauerumschlossenen Höfen.

St. Margarethen, seclusion in walled courtyards.

Wände mit weißem Kalküberzug zum Schutz gegen die Hitze. Scheunenreihen als Verbindung zu Weingarten und Feldern.

Limewashed walls as a protection against heat. Rows of barns as a connecting link to the vineyards and fields.

Klare Trennung von Verkehrsstraße (100) und Wirtschaftsweg (101).

Clear distinction between traffic route (100) and farm tract (101), i.e. main road and accommodation road.

Bauernhäuser in Oslip, deren Ursprung auf das 16.–17. Jh. zurückgeht; meist mit weißem Putz.

Farmhouses at Oslip, originating in the 16th–17th centuries; most of them finished in white plaster.

Hofraum in Mörbisch, dreiseitig von Gebäuden und der Eingangsfront durch Tor umschlossen.

Courtyard at Mörbisch, enclosed on three sides by buildings and by a gate on the entrance side.

Hofgassen in Oslip. Das „menschliche" Maß zwischen niedrigen Häusern, schmalen Gassen und Höfen.

Alleys at Oslip. Low houses, narrow alleys and courtyards preserve the "human" measure.

3. Expressive Architektur

3. Expressive architecture

Es gibt in der Welt Erscheinungen – wie Elemente und Stoffe –, die den Menschen sein ganzes Leben lang umgeben. Das Bauen und Wohnen begleitet ihn durch das ganze Leben. Eine besondere Erwähnung gehört den expressiven Bauwerken, einer ausdrucksvollen und gefühlsbetonten Architektur. Aus dem Zwang regionaler Bedingungen, von äußeren Einflüssen unberührt, im Bauprozeß organisch gewachsen und in der Dynamik landschaftlicher Formen gebaut, scheinen diese Bauwerke mit dem Boden verwachsen zu sein. Die Natur aber besitzt auch andere Entfaltungen als das Bauwerk. Im Aufbau des Skeletts bleibt aber das Gesetzmäßig-–Konstruktive der Architektur wesensverwandt.

Christian Norberg-Schulz, Architekt und Architekturkritiker aus Oslo, schreibt in seinem Essay über „Intentions in Architecture": „Die Freiheit der ‚organischen' Formen, ihr Ausdrucksreichtum, ihr Anpassungsvermögen in den verschiedenen Situationen – all dies wird erst in Verbindung mit der klaren Konstruktion einer technologischen Architektur Wirklichkeit."

Gerade mit der expressiven Architektur wird ein Vorbild geschaffen, das durch Ideenreichtum, stilistische Konsequenz und eine „betonte" Sachlichkeit grundsätzlich Anregungen gibt, die unser Bauen wesentlich mitbestimmen. Die konstruktiv-formal artikulierte Zusammengehörigkeit von Bauelementen als stilbildendes Prinzip führt in ihrer Verschmelzung von Konstruktion und Funktion zu einer architektonischen Logik höherer Ordnung. Die Bedeutung der expressiven Architektur wird im folgenden an drei Prinzipien untersucht:

☐ Intuitive Belebung von Material und Konstruktion

☐ Symbolhaftigkeit in Proportion und Maßstab

☐ Zusammenführung von struktureller räumlicher und flächenhafter Gestalt.

From birth to death man is surrounded by the elements and materials which make up his world. Prominent among these are buildings and particularly the houses in which he lives and has his being. Some of these are expressive structures, emotionally-toned architecture of great power, and merit special mention. Springing from regional conditions, unaffected by extraneous influences, growing organically in the building process and reflecting the dynamics of the landscape, these buildings seem to have risen from the very earth. Nature has many manifestations other than architecture but in the organization of a skeleton building, architecture, based as it is on structural laws, remains very closely linked to the natural world.

Christian Norberg-Schulz, architect and architectural critic from Oslo, writes in his essay on "Intentions in Architecture": "The freedom of 'organic' forms, their rich expressiveness, their adaptability in different situations – all this becomes reality only in conjunction with the clear construction of a technological architecture." It is precisely such expressive architecture that provides us with a model which, through its wealth of ideas, stylistic consistency and "emphatic" functionalism, stimulates our thinking and is an important factor in shaping our buildings. The articulated unity of building elements achieved through the interrelationship of construction and form and constituting a stylistic principle, leads, by amalgamating construction and function, to an architectural logic of a higher order. The importance of expressive architecture will be investigated below by reference to three principles:

☐ Intuitive animation of material and construction

☐ Symbolism in proportion and scale

☐ Unification of spatial and planar design in structure.

Piemontesischer Barock
von Bernardo Antonio Vittone (Italien)
Konstruktion und Ornament

Die Eleganz des italienischen Barock (barocco = unregelmäßig) beruht auf der Linienführung der Struktur (von Säule, Bogen, Pilaster, Giebel usw.), auch wo diese Struktur durch die reiche Ornamentierung verschleiert wird. Die mit Stuck verzierten, kuppelgewölbten Hallenkirchen sind Wunderwerke der Lichtführung und der räumlichen konstruktiven Gestaltung von Rippen und Haut. So stellt etwa die Kuppel von San Lorenzo in Turin (1668–87) den Fall einer architektonischen Vision dar, der die konstruktiven Möglichkeiten der Zeit bis zur äußersten Grenze der Auflockerung des Raumgefüges ausnützte.

Der geniale Baumeister, Bernardo Vittone, hat die Zentralsymmetrie Guarinis übernommen und auf einfache, ländliche Bauten im Piemont übertragen. Es entstanden Räume mit ausgeprägter optischer Wirkung der raumdurchdringenden Bogenelemente: Akzente der Durchdringung und Verschmelzung, des Zusammenführens von Raumteilen, der Aufhebung von vertikalen und horizontalen Begrenzungen.

Piedmontese Baroque
of Bernardo Antonio Vittone (Italy)
Construction and ornament

The elegance of Italian Baroque (barocco = irregular) depends on the design of the structure (pillar, arch, pilaster, gable etc.) even where it is disguised by the rich ornamentation. The hall churches with their stucco ornamentation and domical vaulting are masterpieces in the art of handling light and the spatial constructive design of ribs and skin. Thus, for example, the dome of San Lorenzo in Turin (1668–87) is a case of architectural vision which uses the constructional possibilities of the era to bring the utmost relief to the strict spatial ordonnance.

Bernardo Vittone, that architect of genius, adopted the central symmetry of Guarini and conferred it on simple rural buildings in the Piedmont. Spaces emerged in which the visual impact of arches was particularly marked: penetration and fusion, the bringing together of disparate spaces, the effacement of vertical and horizontal demarcations.

Enges Zusammenwirken von Grund- und Aufriß bei der Verwandlung der statischen Harmonie in eine dynamische Wirklichkeit. Erinnerung an die gewölbten Ausstellungshallen aus vorfabrizierten Betonteilen.
    Flugzeughalle in Orvieto, Pier Luigi Nervi, Rom, 1935–38.

Elevation showing the conversion of static harmony into dynamic reality. Reminiscent of the vaulted exhibition halls of prefabricated concrete elements.
    Aircraft hangar at Orvieto, Pier Luigi Nervi, Rome, 1935–38.

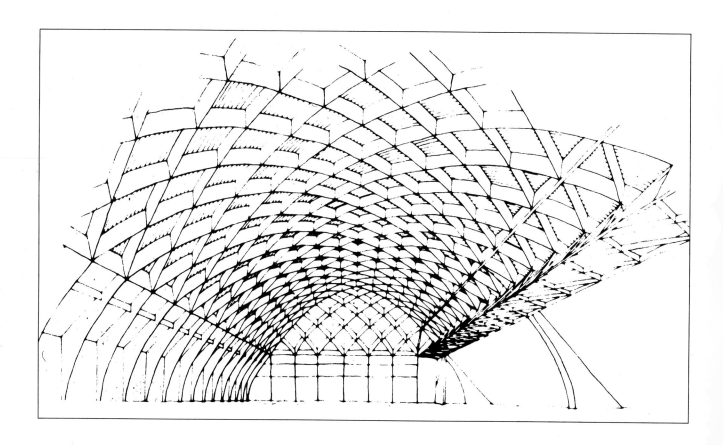

La Capella della Visitazione del Vallinotto,
1738−39.

La Capella della Visitazione del Vallinotto,
1738−39.

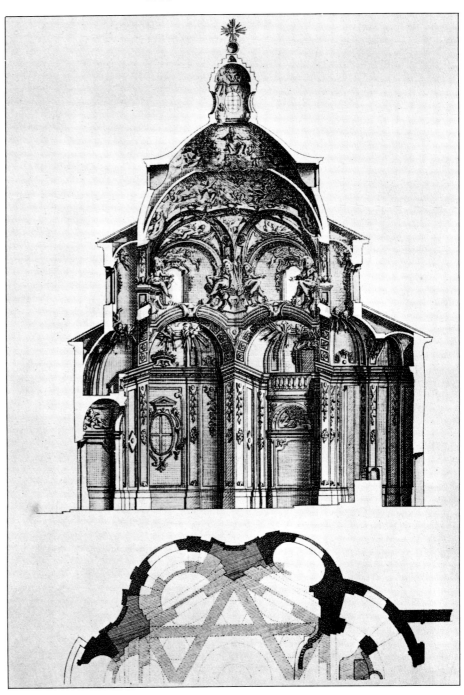

Die Experimente Guarinis wurden vom Piemonte-
ser Vittone in Kleinstädten in volksnahe, bäuerliche
Barockarchitektur umgesetzt.

Guarini's experiments are converted by the Piedmontese Vittone into popular rustic Baroque architecture in small towns.

Bauglieder von konstruktiver Funktion mit flächen-
gebundener Dekoration.

Building elements serving a structural function with
surface decoration.

Piemontesischer Barock von Bernardo Antonio Vittone (Italien)   Piedmontese Baroque of Bernardo Antonio Vittone (Italy)

Sechseckiges Deckengewölbe, reich und farbenfroh dekoriert — ein Höchstmaß an optischer Wirkung.

Hexagonal vaulted ceiling richly decorated in bright colours — the optical effects are maximized.

Chiesa di Santa Chiara di Bra, 1742.
„The undulated wall", organisch, plastisch, geometrisch.

Chiesa di Santa Chiara di Bra, 1742.
"The undulated wall", organic, sculptural, geometric.

Lichteinfall mit Lichtführung im Raumgefüge.   Incident light directed in the structural pattern.

Chiesa di San Luigi Gonzaga del Corteranzo Monferrato, 1738. Eine ellipsenartige Grundform mit Ziegelmauerwerk außen – eine Kolonnade mit kreisförmiger illusionistischer Deckendurchbildung im Innern.

Chiesa di San Luigi Gonzaga del Corteranzo, Monferrato, 1738. A basic elliptoid form with brickwork outside and a colonnade with a circular illusionistic ceiling design inside.

Phantasie und Dynamik im Kuppelgewölbe.   Imagination and vigour in the domical vault.

Klassizistische Architektur in Naantali (Finnland)
Materialwirkung und Formvermögen

Neo-classical architecture at Naantali (Finland)
Effects of material and capacity for form

Die typischen Holzsiedlungen im hohen Norden sind erst im 19. Jh. entstanden. Erst seit der Industrialisierung sind die eigentlichen Städte gegründet worden. Als Baumaterial stand Holz in großen Mengen zur Verfügung. Merkwürdig war, daß sich eine Abart des russischen Klassizismus – der seinerseits von Mitteleuropa nach Rußland gekommen war – in Finnland entwickelte. Das Bedürfnis nach breiteren Straßen, angelegt in einem quadratischen Raster, gab der Planung das Gesicht. Über lange Zeit hat sich das System einstöckiger Holzbauten auf einem Steinsockel in enger Reihung erhalten. Das nordische Tannenholz ist in Ölfarbe imprägniert, wobei Pastelltöne bevorzugt werden, in feiner Nuancierung von Haus zu Haus. Die Fassaden an der Straße zeigen klar gegliederte Fenster und sind mit schmalen Brettern mit Nut und Feder verkleidet. Feine Lisenen in rhythmischer vertikaler Folge beleben die Front. Die einzige Verzierung ist die Fensterumrahmung. Im ganzen ist die Fassade ein klassizistisch einfacher Anblick, wobei das Dach mit seiner schwachen Neigung nicht dominiert. In den Straßenzügen an der Küste Südwestfinnlands ist dieser Holzklassizismus von großer Einfachheit und Schlichtheit heute noch lebendig erhalten.

Carl Ludwig Engel aus Brandenburg (1778–1840), ein Standesgenosse Karl Friedrich Schinkels (1781–1841), kam über Sankt Petersburg 1818 nach Helsinki und prägte dort den neoklassizistischen Stil. Neben den Stadtplänen von Helsinki entwickelte er auch über das ganze Land Zentralkirchen aus Holz, hölzerne Gutshäuser und Gartentempel im klassizistischen Gepräge mit viel Geschmack und Phantasie ohne Schematisierung. Diese strenge und simple Holzarchitektur ist zum Teil auch im nordischen Klima und im finnischen Volkscharakter mit seiner Anerkennung qualitativer Architektur begründet.

The typical timber housing estates in the far north did not emerge until the 19th century, for it was only with the coming of industrialization that actual towns were founded. Because of its abundant supply, wood was the only possible building material. Curiously enough, it was a variant of Russian Classicism, which in turn found its way to Russia from Central Europe, that developed in Finland. The need for broader streets, divided up on a grid, determined the appearance of the planning. For a long time the system of erecting one-storey timber houses on a stone plinth in tight rows persisted. Nordic firwood needs oil paint to impregnate it, and preference was shown for pastel tones which varied slightly in shade from house to house. The street façade has clearly delineated windows and is clad with narrow tongue-and-groove planks. Slender pilaster strips in a rhythmic vertical sequence lend a lively note to the house front. The only decorative feature is the window frame. As a whole the façade is of neo-classical simplicity in its appearance, and the roof, being shallow in pitch, does not dominate. In the streets on the coast of southwest Finland this timber Classicism is of great simplicity and plainness and still retains its vitality today.

Carl Ludwig Engel from Brandenburg (1778–1840), a compeer of Karl Friedrich Schinkel (1781–1841), came to Helsinki via St. Petersburg in 1818 and, all over the country, produced centrally-planned churches of timber, wooden mansion houses and garden temples, neo-classical in style and showing a great deal of taste and imagination without standardization. This severe and simple architecture is also in part a reflection of the Nordic climate and of the Finnish national character in its appreciation of architecture of high quality.

Ideale der griechischen Architektur im Ausdruck
von Tragen und Belasten. Rückgriff auf den Klassizismus wieder im „Post-Modern-Classicism".

Die Architektur des Parthenon belebt Erinne-
rungen an den Klassizismus (Zeichnung von K. Orlandos).

Ideals of Greek architecture in the expression of
pillar and load. Return to Classicism in "Post-
modern Classicism".

The architecture of the Parthenon revives
memories of Classicism (Drawing by K. Orlandos).

Darstellung eines Holzpavillons: Skizze zu Seite
128−129.

A wood pavilion: sketch for the building on pp.
128−129.

Neo-klassizistische Architektur von der Westküste Finnlands, im speziellen vom Städtchen Naantali am bottnischen Meerbusen. Verzicht auf strenge Nüchternheit. Rhythmisierung mit Holzverschalung.

Neo-classical architecture from the west coast of Finland, particularly the little town of Naantali on the Gulf of Bothnia. Strict severity has been abandoned in favour of a rhythmic patterning of the wooden cladding.

Traditionelle Stadthäuser in Holz gegen Ende des 18. Jahrhunderts. Anpassung der Architektur als gebaute stadtlandschaftliche Umwelt.

Traditional town houses of wood of the late 18th century. Adaptation of the architecture as a constructed urban environment.

Maßstäblichkeit am Fensterdetail.　　　　　Scaling in window detail.

Innerstädtischer Bereich einer Kleinstadt Finnlands. Ensemble mit einheitlichen Typen; Sockel aus Steinblöcken; feinmaßstäbliche Aufteilung der Fassaden; leicht geneigtes, vorstehendes Dach mit Metallabdeckung.

Centre of a small town in Finland. Uniformity of type; plinth of stone blocks; finely scaled division of the façades; shallow pitched projecting roof with metal covering.

Die umgebende Natur harmonisiert mit dem Bau-   Natural features harmonize with the structure.
werk.

Haus in Espoo. Linie, Fläche und Volumen bestimmen den neo-klassizistischen Baukörper.

House at Espoo. Line, surface, volume determine the neo-classical building.

Dachformen von Frank Lloyd Wright (USA)
Prägnanz in der Dachform

Um die Jahrhundertwende hatte eine starke Beeinflussung der westlichen Architektur durch die alte fernöstliche Architektur stattgefunden. Es war unter den Architekten vor allem F. L. Wright (1869–1959), der in der japanischen Architektur die Schönheit des aus der Natur erwachsenen Baues, die Bedeutung der Horizontalen und damit die außerordentliche Betonung des Daches entdeckte. Als Beispiel sei nur Wrights Schule in Taliesin (Spring Green, Wisconsin, 1911–25) genannt, die in ihrer baulichen Anlage vor allem die Landschaft integriert. Von ausgeprägter Qualität ist auch die horizontale Gliederung der Dachebene mit dem Gelände des Hauses Jacobs in Wisconsin von 1937. Nach der Jahrhundertwende war es der „europafeindliche" F. L. Wright, der gerade die Präriehäuser, z. B. das frühere Eigenhaus in Oak Park (1889–95) und später das Robie Haus in Chicago (1908–09) mit auskragenden Dächern und die strenge Deckenausbildung des Unitarier-Tempels ebenfalls in Oak Park (1906–07) schuf.

Die Dachgestalt bei Wright erinnert verblüffend an die elementare Steinhütte im Tessin mit bis zur Wiese reichendem Dach: Gebäude Taliesin III, Spring Green, Wisconsin, um 1950.

Gesetzmäßige Anpassung des Maßstabs an seine Umgebung. Baukörper mit dem Hang vereint.

Roof designs by Frank Lloyd Wright (USA)
Terseness in the roof form

At the turn of the century Western architecture came under the marked influence of Oriental styles. Among architects it was mainly Frank Lloyd Wright (1869–1959) who discovered in Japanese architecture the beauty of a building springing from nature, the importance of the horizontal, and hence the extraordinary importance attached to the roof. As an example, reference need only be made to Wright's school at Taliesin (Spring Green, Wisconsin, 1911–25) which, in its architectural layout, is chiefly concerned to integrate with the landscape. In the Jacobs house in Wisconsin of 1937, the horizontal organization of the roof plane to extend the house into the landscape is also of superb quality.

After the turn of the century it was the "Europhobe" F. L. Wright who produced the prairie houses, exemplified by his own earlier house at Oak Park (1889–95), and later the Robie house in Chicago (1908–09) with the cantilevered roofs, and the severely simple arrangement of the ceilings in the Unity Temple, also in Oak Park (1906–07).

There is an astonishing resemblance between the ▷ roof of Wright's building and that of the stone hut in Ticino which reaches down to the grass. Building at Taliesin III, Spring Green, Wisconsin, c. 1950.

Ordered adaptation of the scale to the environment. The building is unified with the slope.

Umfassende Einheit zwischen Material und Konstruktion. Der Raum ist mit der Landschaft verbunden.

Alte, heute noch intakte Gestalt einer Steinhütte im Verzascatal, Tessin.

Complete unity between material and construction. Enclosed and landscape unified.

Traditional vernacular architecture; still intact stone hut in the Val Verzasca, Ticino.

Haus W. W. Willits, Highland Park, Illinois, 1902.
Das Plattendach mit niedrigen, horizontalen Flü-
geln bestimmen das Bauwerk.

W. W. Willits house, Highland Park, Illinois, 1902.
The sheet roof with low horizontal wings determines
the structure.

Unitarier-Kirche, Madison, Wisconsin, 1949. Dachfläche mit Kupferverkleidung aus regelmäßig aneinandergefügten Streifen.

Nach Wright bedeutet das Quadrat Integrität, der Kreis Unendlichkeit und das Dreieck Streben.

Unitarian Church, Madison, Wisconsin, 1949. Roof surface with copper cladding in regular strips.

According to Wright the square indicates integrity, the circle infinity and the triangle effort.

Haus Jacobs, Madison, Wisconsin, 1937. Überraschende Lösung eines einstöckigen Flachdachhauses: Die horizontalen hölzernen Attiken sind in das Gelände eingepaßt.

Jacobs house, Madison, Wisconsin, 1937. Surprising design of a one-storey flat-roofed house: the horizontal wood roof parapets are fitted into the terrain.

Unity Temple, Oak Park, Illinois, 1906. Giganti-
sches Rahmenwerk von Oberlichtern in geometri-
scher Strenge. Das überscharfe Licht wird durch das
getönte Glas gebrochen.

Unity Temple, Oak Park, Illinois, 1906. Giant
framework of skylights in a strict geometrical
pattern. The excessively bright light is strained by
the tinted glass.

Schrifttum / Bibliography

Abschnitt/Part II/1:

Le Village des Bories à Gordes dans le Vaucluse (Katalog) 1976.

Edward Allen: Stone Shelters. The MIT Press, Cambridge, 1969.

Ludwig Bieler: Irland. Urs Graf Verlag, Olten, 1961.

Merian (Monatsheft): Irland. Hoffmann und Campe Verlag, Hamburg, 1959.

Museo Walser: (Katalog) Alagna Valsesia, 1979.

Hans Soeder: Urformen der abendländischen Baukunst. Du Mont Dokumente, Köln, 1964.

Abschnitt/Part II/2:

Francisc Nistor: Sculptura si Arhitectura Populara din Zona, Etnografica, Maramures, Baia-Mare, 1969.

D. N. Goberman: Wooden architectural Monuments of Trans-Carpathia. Aurora Art Publishers, Leningrad, 1970.

Bernard Rudofsky: Architecture Without Architects. The Museum of Modern Art, New York, 1964.

Franz Simon: Bäuerliche Bauten im Südburgenland. (Selbstverlag) A-7432 Obersützen, 1971.

Roland Rainer: Anonymes Bauen im Nordburgenland. Verlag Galerie Welz, Salzburg, 1961.

Abschnitt/Part II/3:

Bernardo Vittone: Architetto (Catalogo) Città di Vercelli, 1967.

Pierre Charpentrat: Barock. Office du Livre, Fribourg, 1964.

Thérèse und Jean-Marie Bresson: Frühe skandinavische Holzhäuser. Beton-Verlag, Düsseldorf, 1981.

Bruno Zevi: Frank Lloyd Wright. Verlag für Architektur, Zürich, 1980.

F. L. Wright: The Robie House, Prairie School Press, Chicago, 1968.

Nachweis der Zeichnungen / Sources of drawings

 33 Le Village des Bories à Gordes
 57 Museo Walser Freilichtmuseum in Alagna
 71 Volkskunde Museum in Sighetu Marmatiei, Maramures
 95 Anonymes Bauen Nordburgenland, von Roland Rainer
109 Bernardo Vittone, Architetto, Città di Vercelli
121 Unto Aarnio: Naantalista. Aurajoen Kirjapaino OY Turku, 1978.

Index

Alagna 56—67
Alpi d'Otro 65—67
Aran 44—53
Ascona 26—27

Barfüsserplatz 20—21
Basel 10—11, 20—21, 24—25
Bern 22—23
Bristol 70
Budeşti 76
Burgenland 94—105

Caldwell, A. 70
Chicago 18
Corteranzo 116
Cosâutal 76

Espoo 130—131

Florisdorf 12—13

Galway Bay 45
Gordes 31—43
Guarini 107, 110

Helsinki 120
Highland Park 134

Inisheer 46
Izatal 72

Jacobs 138—139
Jahn, H. 18—19
Jeannert, P. 57
Jeud 72

Kurrent, F. 12—13
Küsnacht 14—15

Le Corbusier 57, 68, 82—83, 91
Locarno 16—17
Lüber, J. 32

Madison 138—139
Maramureş 69—81
Mies van der Rohe, L. 44—45, 68
Minnesota 18—19
Monferrato 116—119
Mörbisch 103
Moser, K. 24—25
Murphy, C. F. 18—19

Naantali 120—129
Nervi, P. L. 108
Norberg-Schulz, Ch. 106

Oak Park 140—141
Orvieto 108
Oslip 96—97, 102, 104

Piemont 107—119

Ronchamp 83
Robie House 132
Rozavlea 80

Spalt, J. 12
Stromboli 82—93
St. Margarethen 98

Taliesin 132—133
Trausdorf 95

Unitarian Church 136—137
Unity Temple 140—141
Universität Basel 10—11

Vacchini, L. 16—17
Vallinotto 109—113
Valsesia 56
Vaucluse 31
Verzascatal 133
Vittone, B. 107—119
Vischer, F. 10—11

Walser-Häuser 56—67
Weber, G. 10—11
Wright, F. L. 132—141
Willits, W. W. 134—135
Wien 12—13